Salty Breeze
Boats & Ships Coloring Book

Color Sea Vessels, Fishing Boats, Yachts, Cruise Liners, Sailing Ships – For Adults

Rachel Mintz

Images used under license from Shutterstock.com

Copyright © 2018 Palm Tree Publishing - All rights reserved.
No part of this publication may be reproduced, distributed, or transmitted in any form or by any means, including photocopying, recording, or other electronic or mechanical methods, without the prior written permission of the publisher, except in the case of brief quotations embodied in critical reviews and certain other noncommercial uses permitted by copyright law.

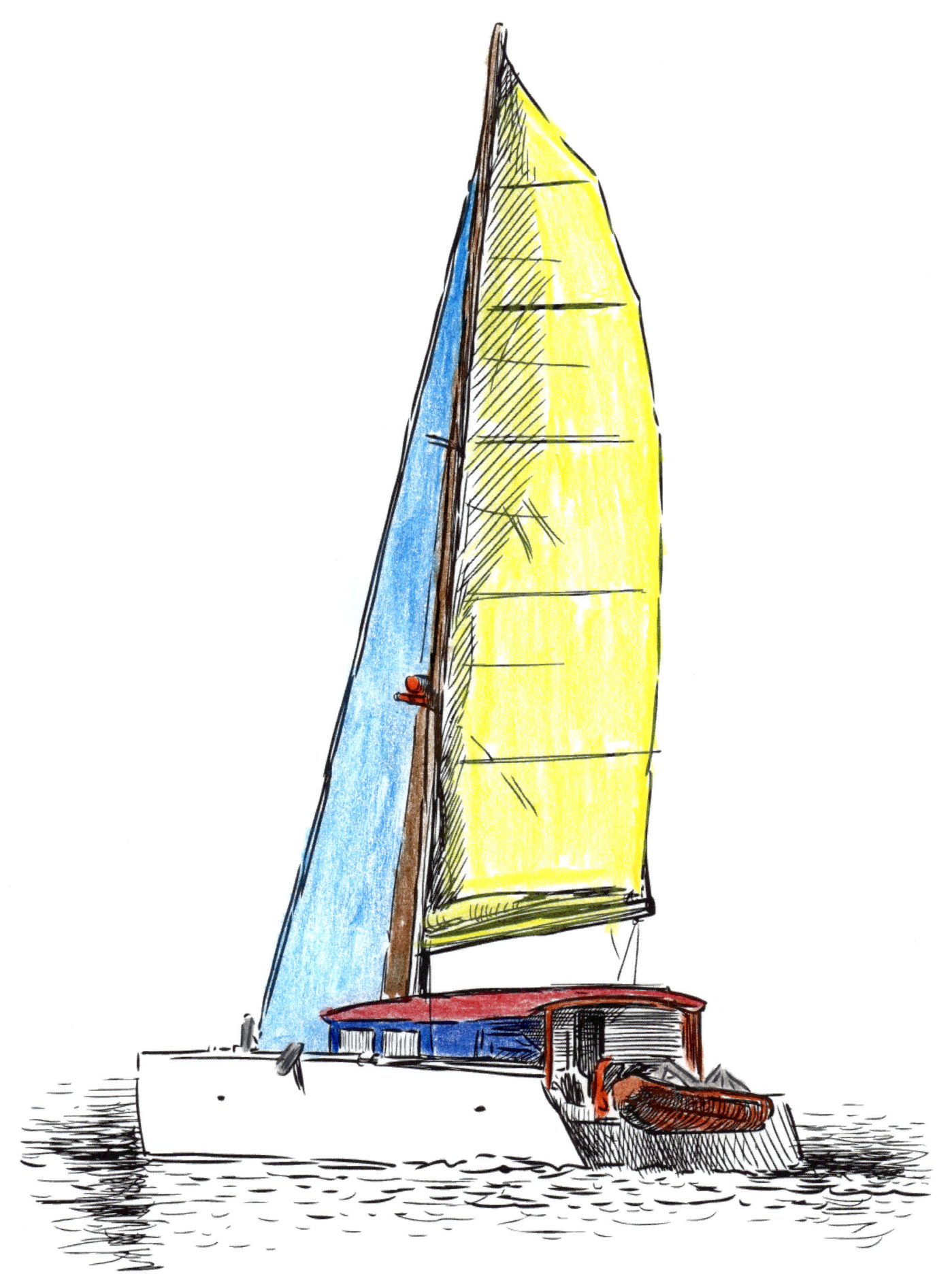

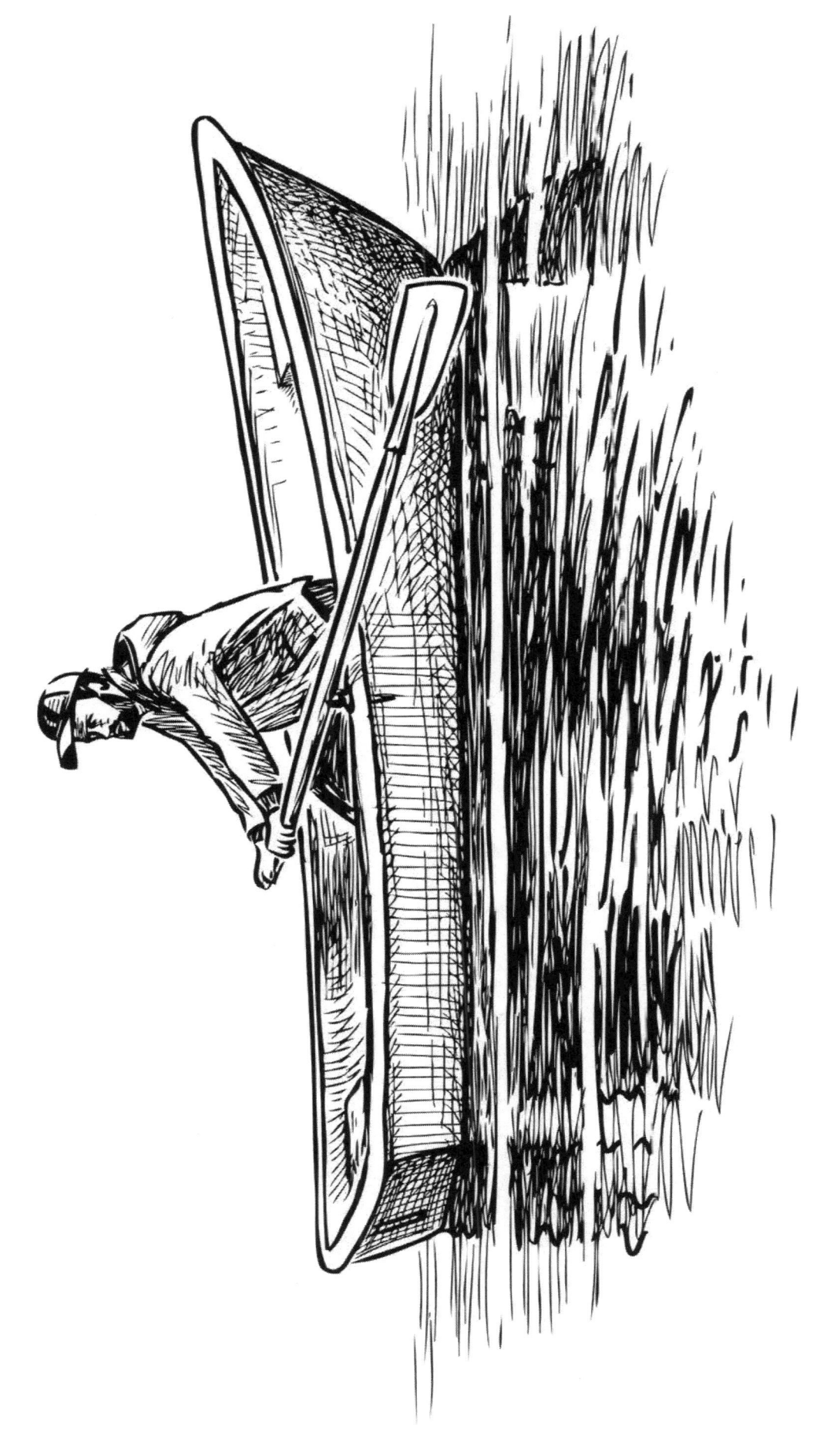

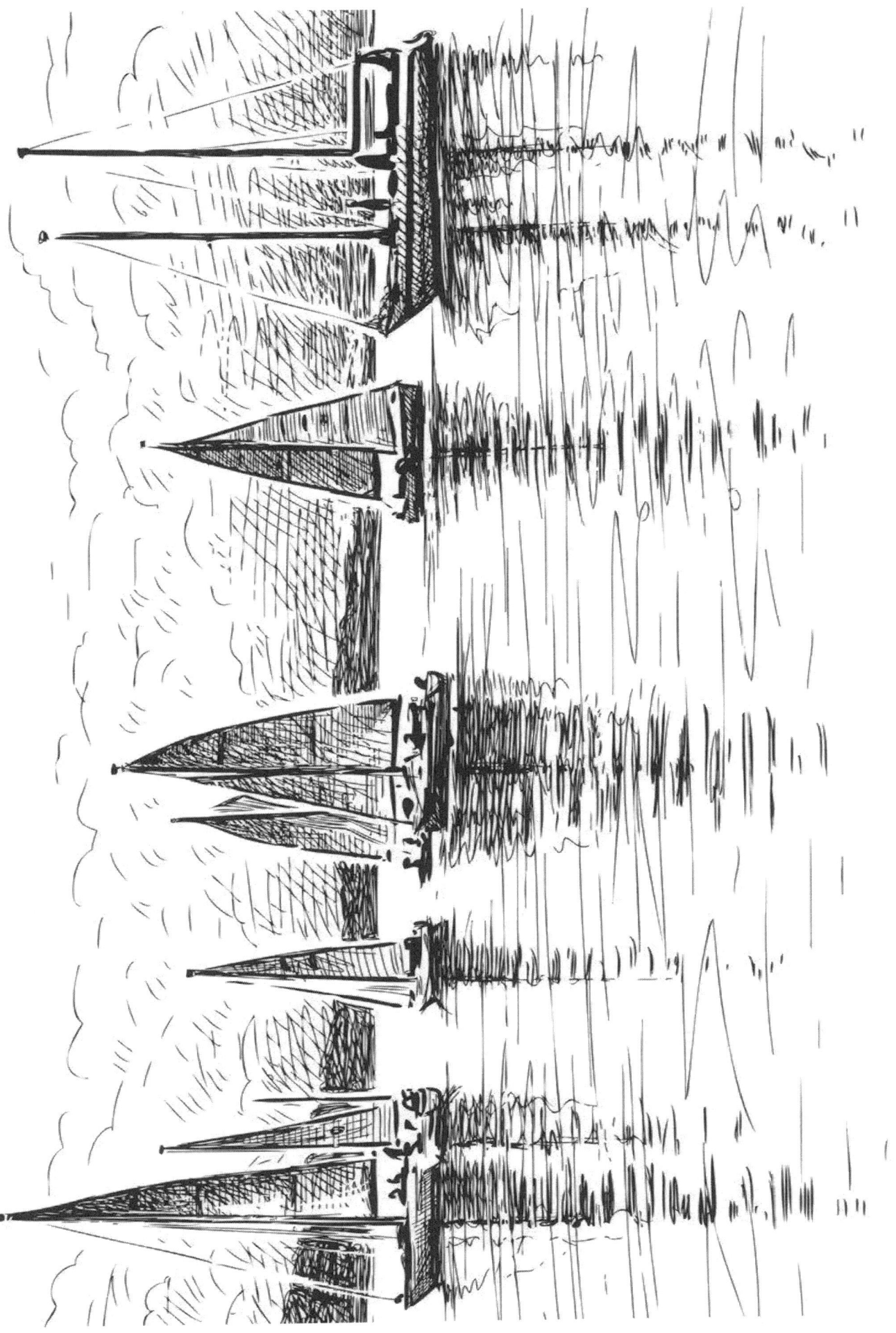

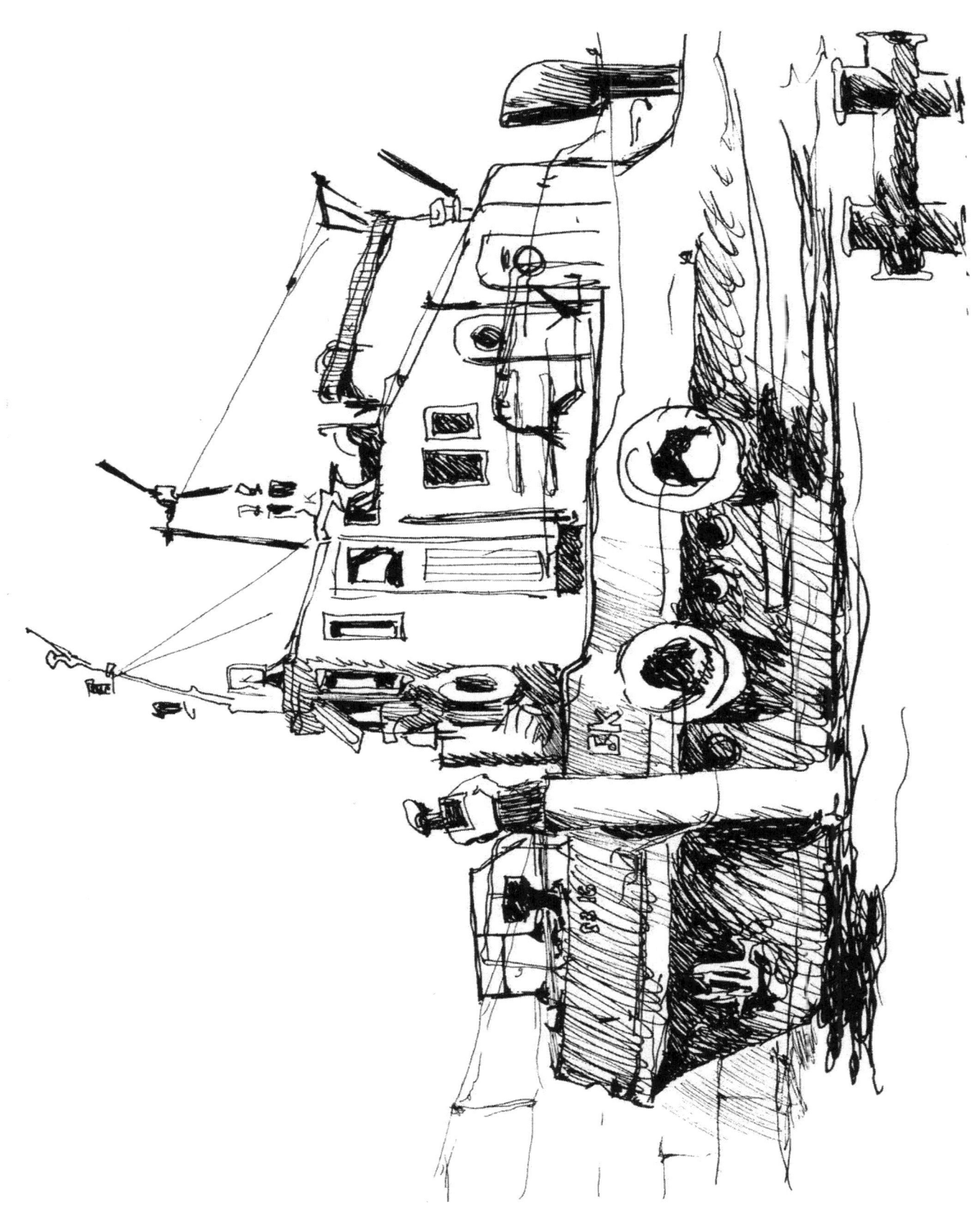

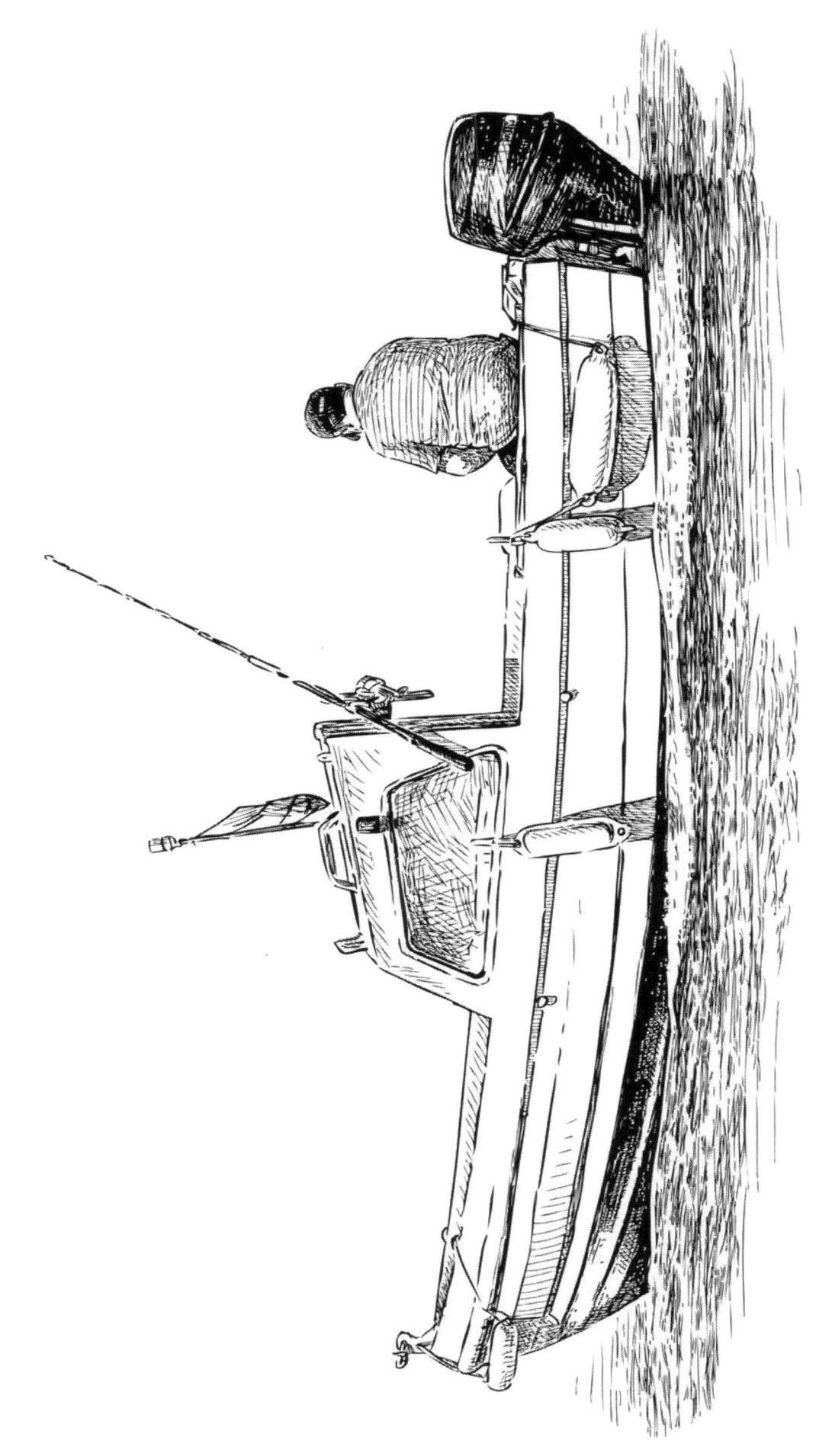

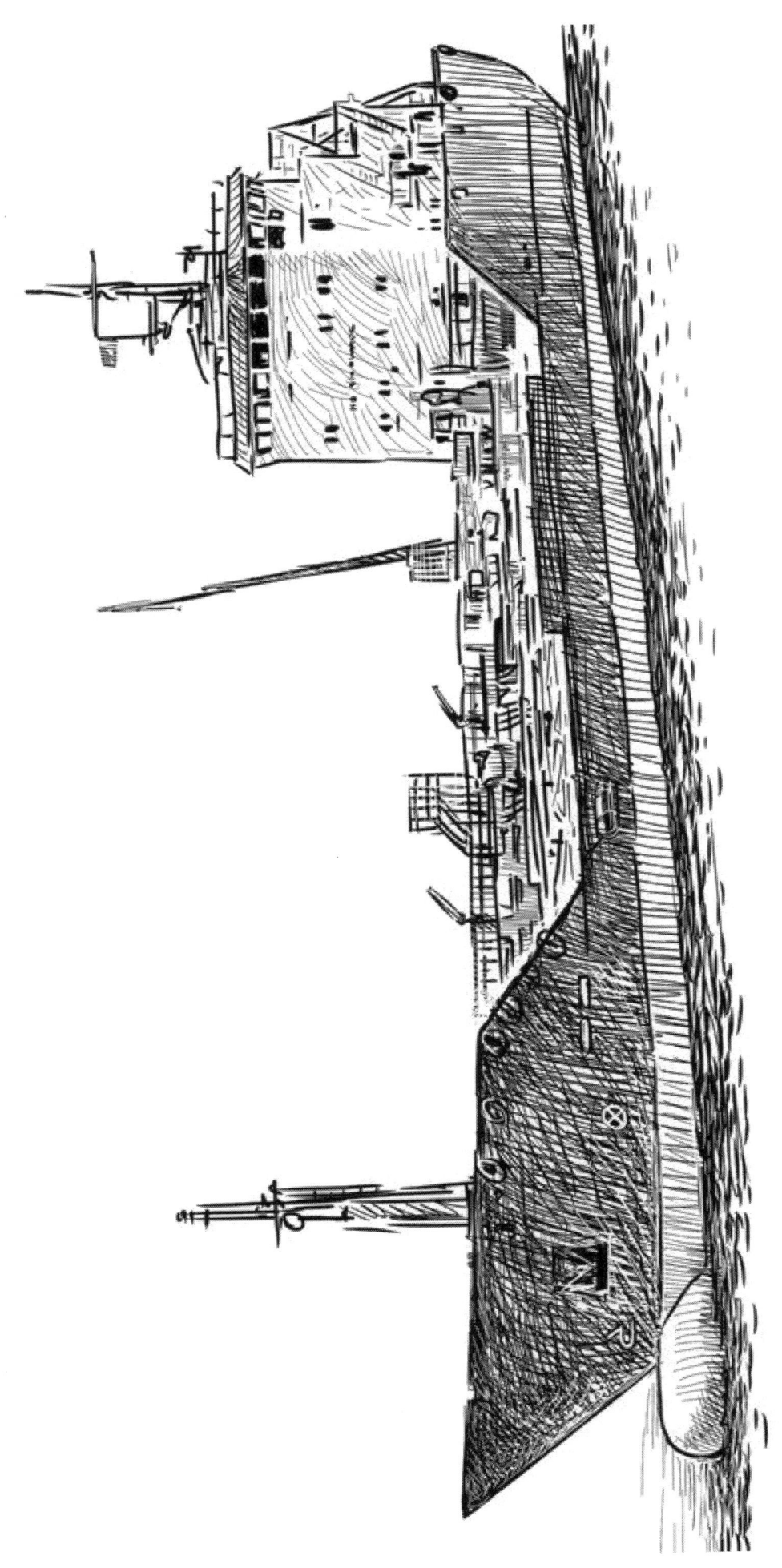

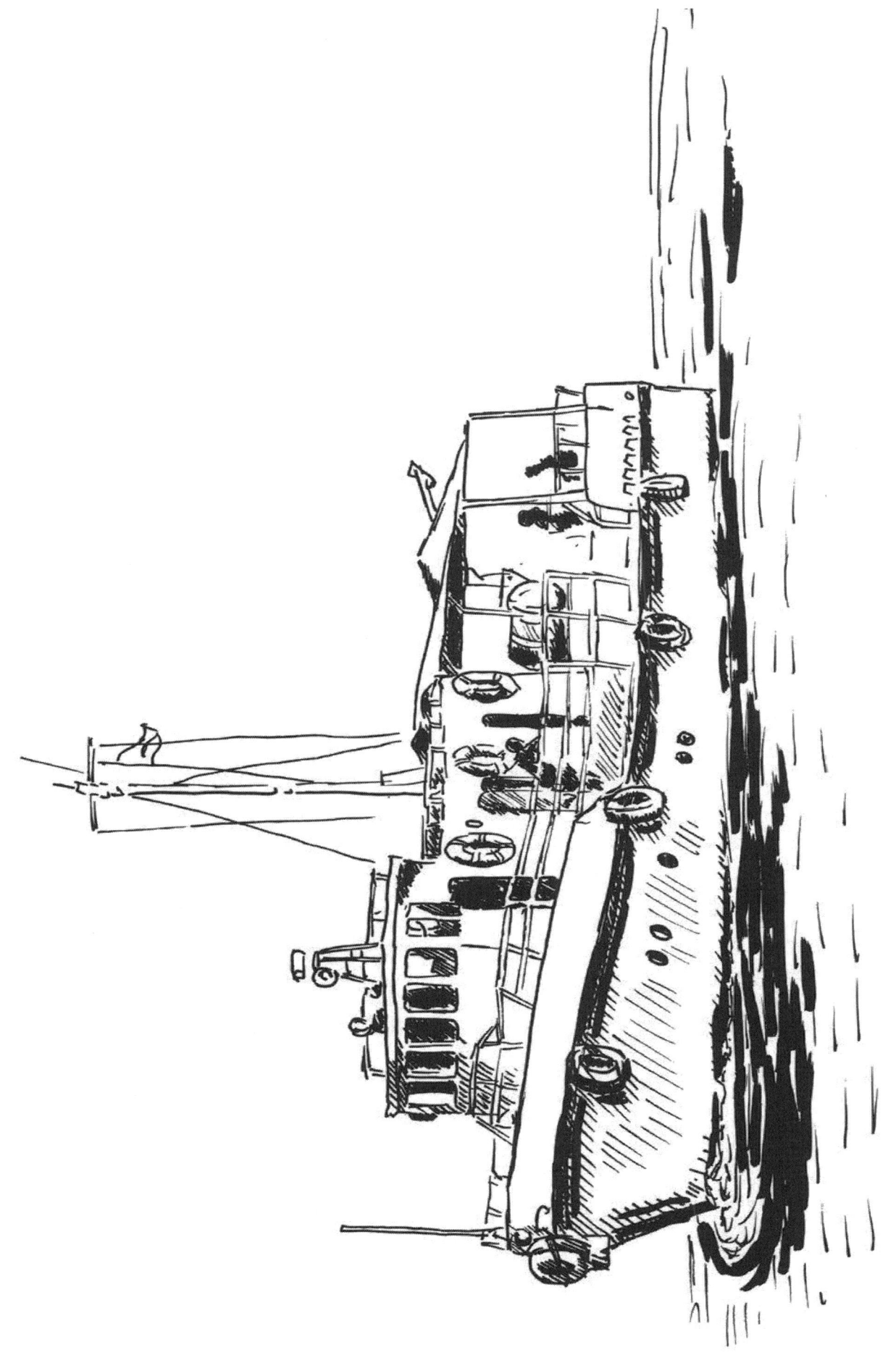

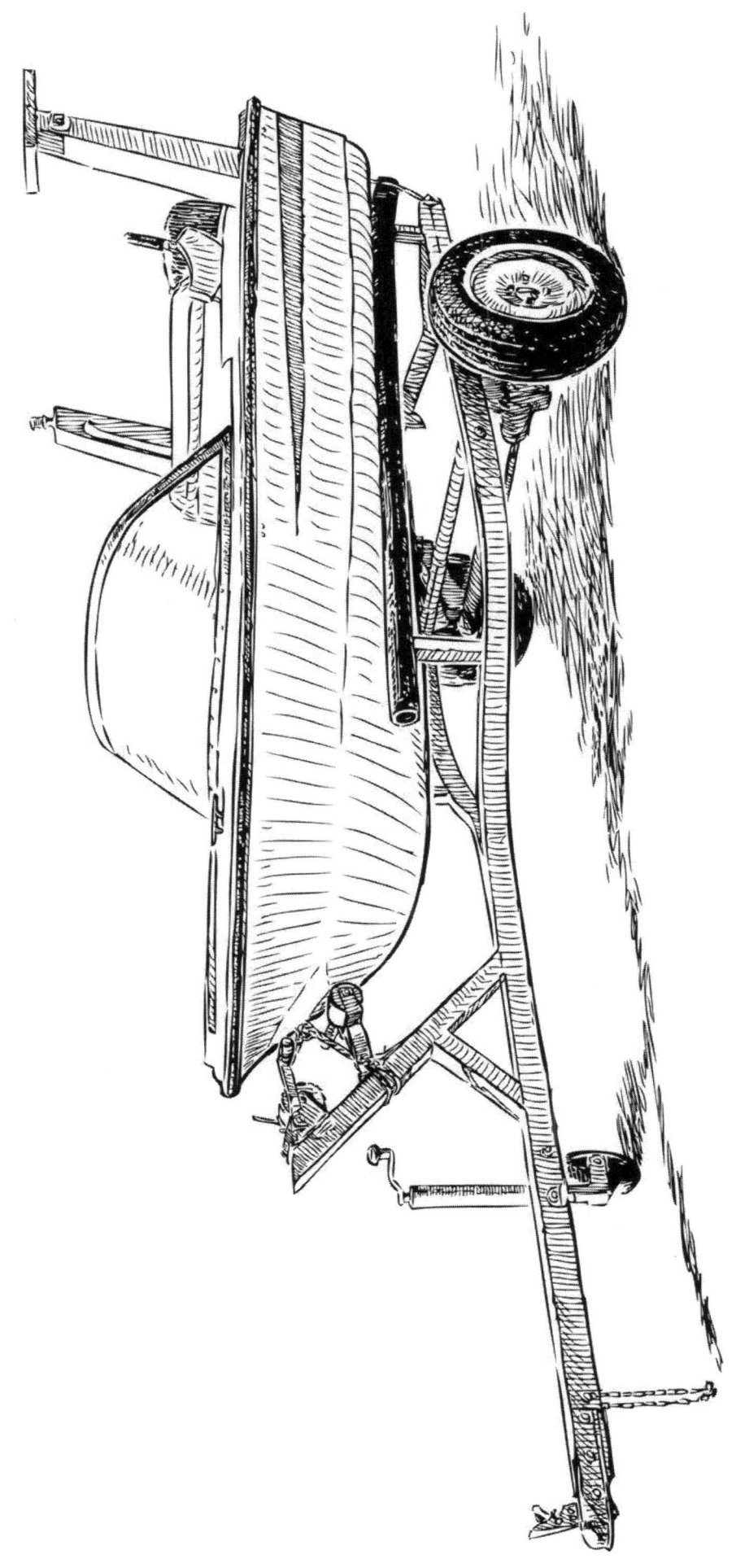

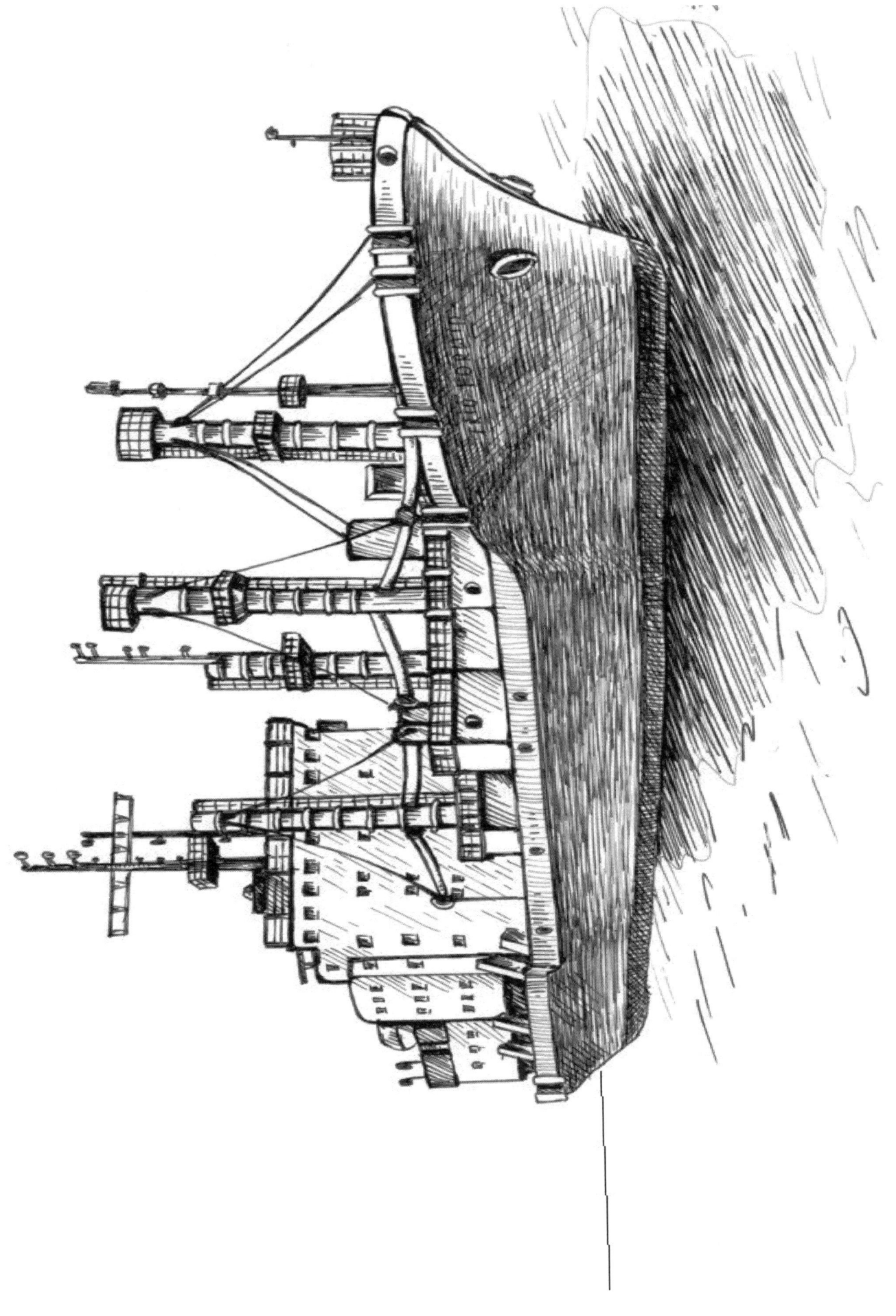

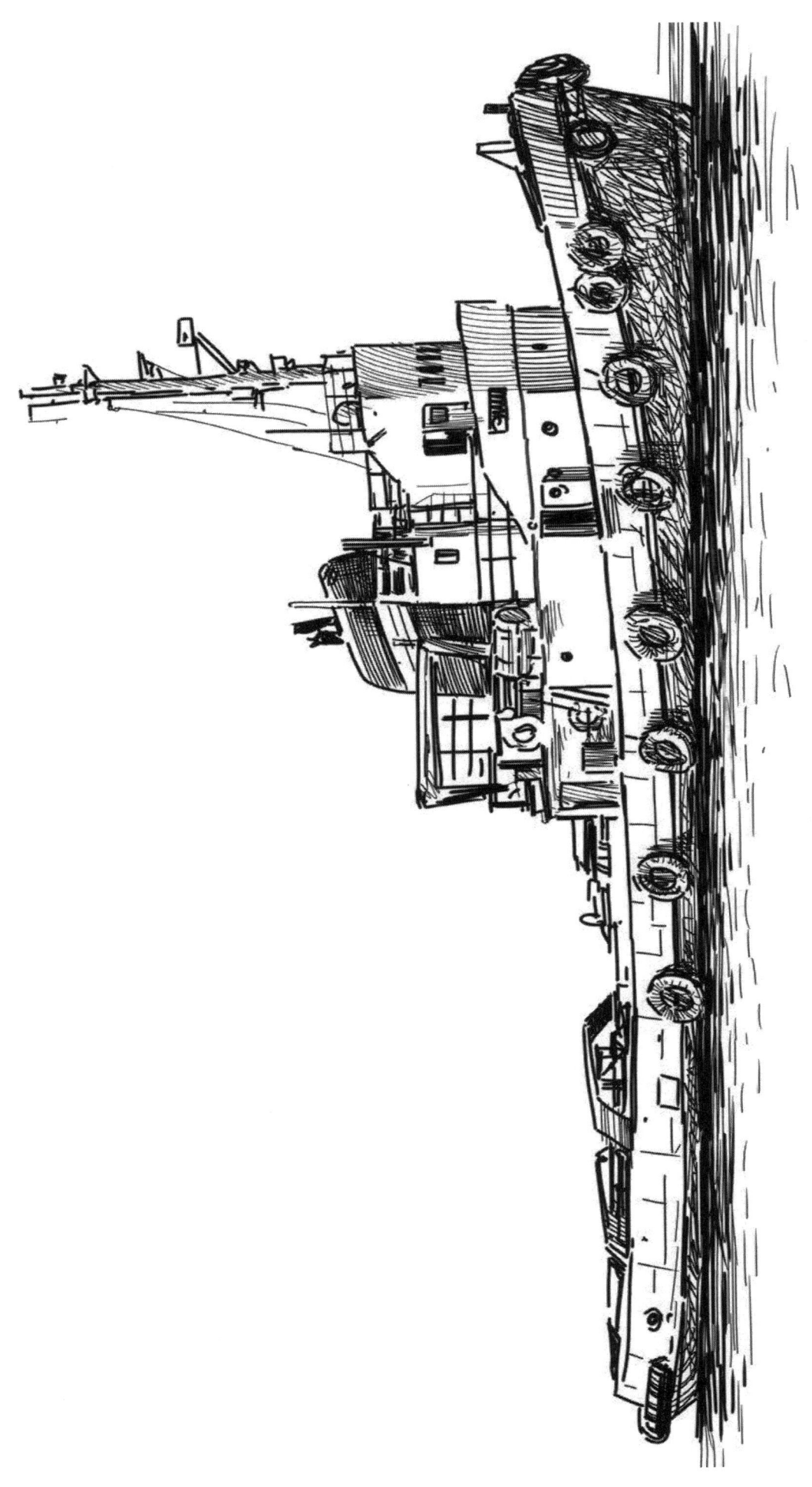

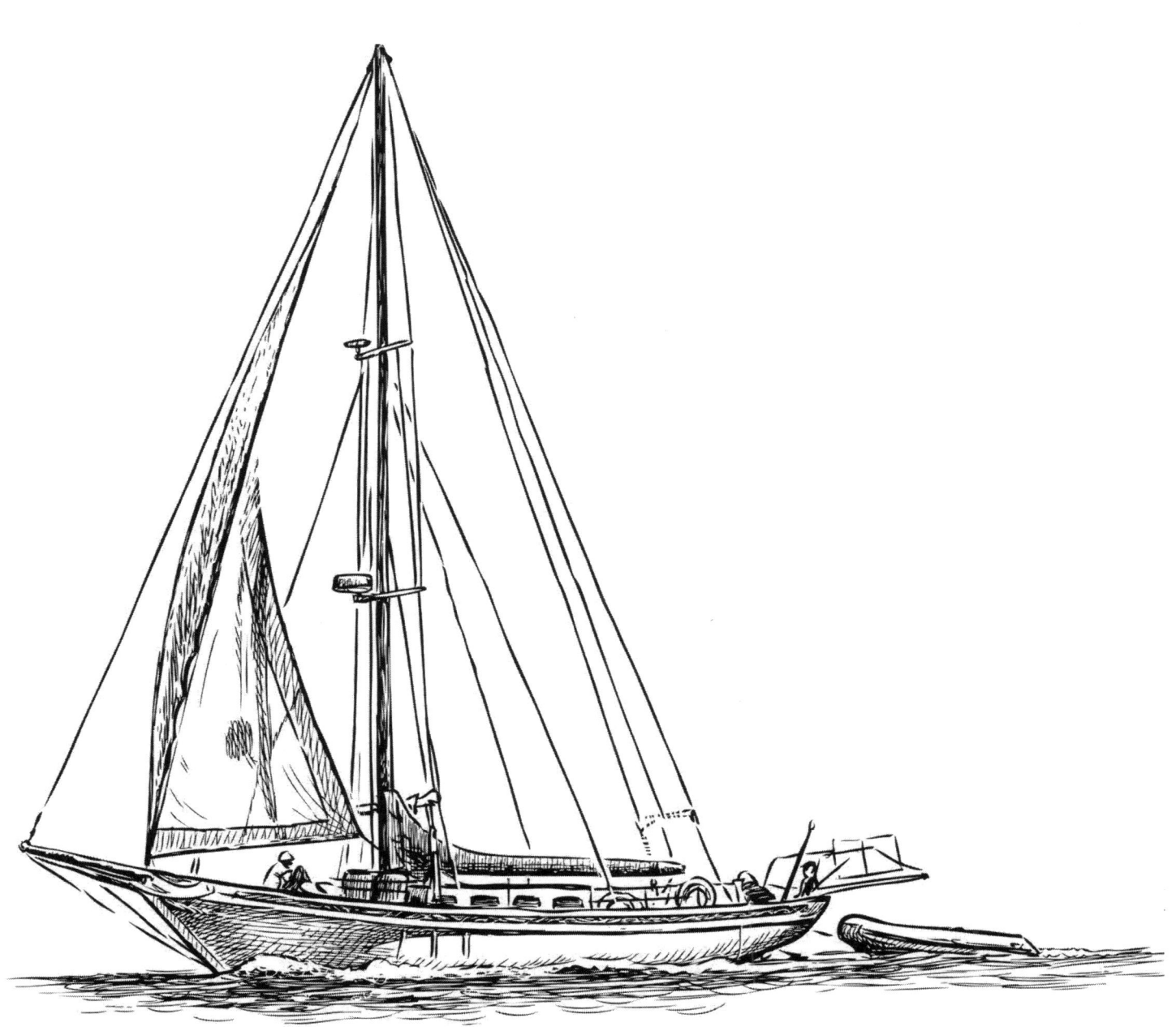

Thank you for coloring with us

Please consider to rate & review

More from our coloring books:

Rachel Mintz

Countryside Houses
Coloring Book For Adults

Trees
Coloring Book

Thank you for coloring with us

Made in the USA
Middletown, DE
14 June 2022